THIRTIETH YEAR
TO HEAVEN
New American Poets

THIRTIETH YEAR TO HEAVEN

NEW AMERICAN POETS

Doug Abrams
Barbara Friend
Maria Ingram
Kate Jennings
Robert Schultz

FIVE POEMS WITH COMMENTARY BY

A. R. Ammons
John Hollander
Josephine Jacobsen
Josephine Miles
Robert Penn Warren

Photographs by Susan Mullally Weil

The Brée Books
Number 2

The Jackpine Press   Winston-Salem, N.C.   1980

Library of Congress Cataloging in Publication Data
Thirtieth Year to heaven.

(The Brée books; no. 2)
1. American poetry--20th century. I. Abrams,
Doug. II. Series: Brée books; no. 2.
PS615.T48   811'.5' 08   80–22063
ISBN 0–917492–09–9

ACKNOWLEDGMENTS

Grateful acknowledgment is made to the following for permission to reprint previously published material:

Title and Epigraph, from *The Poems* of Dylan Thomas, Copyright 1946, NEW DIRECTIONS.

Ammons, A. R.: "Hymn" from *Collected Poems 1951–1971*, Copyright 1972, W. W. NORTON & COMPANY, INC.

Hollander, John: "The Lady's-Maid's Song" from *A Crackling of Thorns* by John Hollander, Copyright 1958, YALE UNIVERSITY PRESS; in *Spectral Emanations* by John Hollander, Copyright 1978, ATHENEUM PUBLISHERS.

Jacobsen, Josephine: "Let Each Man Remember" from *Let Each Man Remember*, Copyright 1940, THE KALEIDOGRAPH PRESS; in *The Shade-Seller*, Copyright 1974, DOUBLEDAY & COMPANY, INC.

Miles, Josephine: "For Futures" from *Lines at Intersection*, Copyright 1939, The MACMILLAN COMPANY; in *Poems/1930–1960*, Copyright 1960, INDIANA UNIVERSITY PRESS.

Warren, Robert Penn: "The Return: An Elegy" from THE ALCESTIS PRESS, Copyright 1935; NEW DIRECTIONS, Copyright 1942; in *Selected Poems 1923–1943*, Copyright 1944, HARCOURT, BRACE AND COMPANY; in *Selected Poems 1923–1975*, Copyright 1976 by Robert Penn Warren, RANDOM HOUSE, INC.

Acknowledgments and copyrights continue at the back of this book, on page 140 and 141, an extension of the copyright page.

It was my thirtieth
Year to heaven stood there then in the summer noon
Though the town below lay leaved with October blood.
O may my heart's truth
Still be sung
On this high hill in a year's turning.

— Dylan Thomas:
"Poem in October"

Preface

Thirtieth Year to Heaven is an anthology of poetry written during the "summer noon" of youth celebrated in "Poem in October" by Dylan Thomas. It includes the work of five new American poets, whose experiences range from driving trucks in Iowa to riding tobacco sleds in North Carolina. Now their careers are those of teachers, lawyers, shopkeepers, counselors, and parents. They regard the writing of poetry as central in their lives, and are publishing in journals and chapbooks and participating in workshops and readings. The Jackpine Press is proud to present these poets to a large audience with confidence that they have energies and talents for sustained achievement in the years ahead.

Doug Abrams, Barbara Friend, Maria Ingram, Kate Jennings, and Robert Schultz have chosen for inclusion in this volume favorite older American poets. Three of them — Jacobsen, Miles, and Warren — have been writing for a half-century; two others, Ammons and Hollander, have passed the half-century mark in age. Warren and Miles have retired from full-time university teaching, Jacobsen is a frequent lecturer on campuses, and Ammons and Hollander direct writing programs at Cornell and Yale. If these younger poets sometimes feel their energies dissipated in work unrelated to poetry, they can recall the career of Ammons, who at their ages was far afield working as an executive in a glass-manufacturing firm, or of Jacobsen, who was often preoccupied with the demands of home and family.

Each of the older poets has chosen a single poem from the work of early years and has written a commentary about the importance of this poem as pivotal in shaping a career, or as establishing the themes which earlier poems had introduced and later poems would develop. Whether giving the poet "a base for the future," as Warren describes the significance of his poem, or "a turning point, a new hope, a place to come back to," as Ammons accounts for his selection, these poems return the poets to their sources.

As the five older poets look back to poems written during their own summer noon and as the younger poets look ahead, hopeful of a

x   place in the ranks, readers may find unities and continuities in these poems of young men and women of different generations.

We invite you to come to a "high hill in a year's turning" and enjoy *Thirtieth Year to Heaven*.

Contents

II
THE LAST STRIPTEASE
Barbara Friend

III
THE BRIDEGROOM OF MYTILINI
Maria Ingram

IV
PROVOCATION
Kate Jennings

V
THE QUARRY
Robert Schultz

Part One

FIVE POEMS

A. R. AMMONS

Hymn

I know if I find you I will have to leave the earth
and go on out
   over the sea marshes and the brant in bays
and over the hills of tall hickory
and over the crater lakes and canyons
and on up through the spheres of diminishing air
past the blackset noctilucent clouds
      where one wants to stop and look
way past all the light diffusions and bombardments
up farther than the loss of sight
   into the unseasonal undifferentiated empty stark

And I know if I find you I will have to stay with the earth
inspecting with thin tools and ground eyes
trusting the microvilli sporangia and simplest
   coelenterates
and praying for a nerve cell
with all the soul of my chemical reactions
and going right on down where the eye sees only traces

You are everywhere partial and entire
You are on the inside of everything and on the outside

I walk down the path down the hill where the sweetgum
has begun to ooze spring sap at the cut
and I see how the bark cracks and winds like no other bark
chasmal to my ant-soul running up and down
and if I find you I must go out deep into your
   far resolutions
and if I find you I must stay here with the separate leaves

ৼ৾ ৾ঽ

    I started writing my "Ezra" poems while Phyllis and I were living
in Berkeley, California, and while I was doing some academic work in

4

English. In 1952 we returned to live in South Jersey and I began to work at the glass factory. I had difficult years of adjusting and couldn't write. One day in April I met Dr. Theodore E. Weichselbaum of St. Louis, a brilliant man who became my most-prized business associate. The day after meeting him and talking amateurish — on my part — big talk about science (the mechanistic versus the vitalistic views of things) I loved so much, I found myself going upstairs to the typewriter after dinner feeling that I had a poem in balance in my hands that I might drop, lose the tone of. But I went on up and "Hymn" came out almost verbatim as it is. It felt like a renewal and recommencement for me. It was a turning point, a new hope, a place to come back to.

— A.R.A.

JOHN HOLLANDER

The Lady's-Maid's Song

When Adam found his rib was gone
   He cursed and sighed and cried and swore
And looked with cold resentment on
   The creature God had used it for.
All love's delights were quickly spent
   And soon his sorrows multiplied:
He learned to blame his discontent
   On something stolen from his side.

And so in every age we find
   Each Jack, destroying every Joan,
Divides and conquers womankind
   In vengeance for his missing bone.
By day he spins out quaint conceits
   With gossip, flattery, and song,
But then at night, between the sheets,
   He wrongs the girl to right the wrong.

Though shoulder, bosom, lip, and knee
   Are praised in every kind of art,
Here is love's true anatomy:
   His rib is gone; he'll have her heart.
So women bear the debt alone
   And live eternally distressed,
For though we throw the dog his bone
   He wants it back with interest.

⁍ ⁞

I wrote this song when I was 22 years old, as one of a number of lyrics — and a very Drydenesque Prologue and Epilogue — for a production of a Restoration Comedy, Sir George Etherege's *The Man of Mode* at Barnard College. At one point, one of the heroines sweeps off stage with a threat, which neither she nor the audience believes, to give up the erotic life forever and immure herself in a convent. Here a change of scene was required, and we arranged for her *confidante* to come down to the footlights before a drop and, "in one" as they say in the theatre, sing the above. She starts out from a high, neutral, sceptical position, but in the last quatrain the "we" makes it clear that her intent is complaint rather than commentary on Genesis. The music, and the production of the play, have long since faded, but I reprinted the text in my first book of poems, and I still read it aloud from time to time; it's the earliest-written verse of mine that I ever use at readings.

Aside from the dramatic exigencies of this occasion, and the allusively archaized diction, I wrote many quasi-songs (what Yeats called "words for music perhaps") for particular personae at that time. I felt not only the formal influence of Yeats and Auden (a cancelled version of one line originally went "And then at night, between the sheets,/ Seeks to regain that missing bone," which was pure Crazy Jane), but a particular moral mandate. Men of imagination ought to try to frame a feminist view, and vice versa—after all, moral imagination consists partly in being able to imagine what it's like to be someone else. The war between men and women is fought in the darkened valleys of imaginative failure. So that I was very serious "about" this playful song, not implicitly bitching up the singer (and thereby her sex) for seizing on the synecdoche of the rib, but rather sharing the delight of the maid — and the old-fashioned *femme-savante* sort of folklore she was purveying — in discovering that particular loophole in the available mythology.

— J.H.

JOSEPHINE JACOBSEN

Let Each Man Remember

There is a terrible hour in the early morning
When men awake and look on the day that brings
The hateful adventure, approaching with no less certainty
Than the light that grows, the untroubled bird that sings.

It does not matter what we have to consider,
Whether the difficult word, or the surgeon's knife,
The last silver goblet to pawn, or the fatal letter,
Or the prospect of going on with a particular life.

The point is, they rise; always they seem to have risen,
(They always will rise, I suppose) by courage alone.
Somehow, by this or by that, they engender courage,
Courage bred in flesh that is sick to the bone.

Each in his fashion, they compass their set intent
To rout the reluctant sword from the gripping sheath,
By thinking, perhaps, upon the Blessed Sacrament,
Or perhaps by coffee, or perhaps by gritted teeth.

It is indisputable that some turn solemn or savage,
While others have found it serves them best to be glib,
When they inwardly lean and listen, listen for courage,
That bitter and curious thing beneath the rib.

With nothing to gain, perhaps, and no sane reason
To put up a fight, they grip and hang by the thread
As fierce and still as a swinging threatened spider.
They are too brave to say, It is simpler to be dead.

Let each man remember, who opens his eyes to that morning,
How many men have braced them to meet the light,
And pious or ribald, one way or another, how many
Will smile in its face, when he is at peace in the night.

~§ §~

    Acutely aware of how often early poems, in later analysis, are made
to bear a weight of implication they cannot sustain, I approach "Let
Each Man Remember" with caution.

I have selected it for three reasons: It is a very early poem, written as I was first beginning to publish poetry. It was a poem written under extreme emotional pressure; and it is a poem in which I think I can detect, without rationalizing, most of the directions of my later poetry. By choosing a poem written at so early a stage of one's profession, it is easier to spot the weaknesses to be overcome, the emotional bias, and any latent strengths. A poem written under emotional pressure will present in its sharpest aspects the problem of form versus self-indulgence. And a poem which contains the seeds of subsequent development will tell whether there has been a general direction, however diversified the approaches.

Weaknesses of this poem, as I now see it, are a monotony of rhythm, (though this is not total) and a certain hortatory accent. On the second point, that of emotional pressure, the poem succeeds, I think, in breeding a passionately-felt emotion with an elected form, and in the realization of a community of predicament — two indications of self-discipline which argue well for the future. There is a sparsity of adjectives and a frequency of tough-textured words (hateful, knife, rise, bred, bone, rout, gritted, savage, glib, bitter, rib, fight, grip, hang, fierce, ribald), an approach which is going to shape future ideas of durable structure.

As to the concerns — they are with people, with human beings in various conditions of stress; with the active as against the passive, (even the still, threatened spider grips and hangs and is fierce); with humor in some form — glib, ribald — as the saving particle; with the presence of death, first as a rejected alternative, last as a universal solvent. The whole body of my subsequent poetry has been bred out of similar encounters, and it is these which have led, recently, to my fiction. Human time is in "Let Each Man Remember," between the two silences which bracket it. There is a native suspicion of the pompous, and of the ego's grandiloquent self-pity.

The whole world of exploration into the possibilities of technique and innovation is still ahead — that endless series of discoveries which can revolutionize, again and again, the daring approach to a poem, while the center holds constant.

And *any* lines which can give their begetter satisfaction after decades roll up, are a rarity. I still think of courage as
that bitter and curious thing beneath the rib.

—J.J.

JOSEPHINE MILES

For Futures

When the lights come on at five o'clock on the street corners
That is Evolution by the bureau of power,
That is a fine mechanic dealing in futures:
For the sky is wide and warm upon that hour,

But like the eyes that burned once at sea bottom,
Widening in the gloom, prepared for light,
The ornamental standards, the glazed globes softly
Perceive far off how probable is night.

⟜§ §⟝

Compared to poems of today, even many of my own, this poem seems compressed, an atmosphere focused into a concept. I hoped to catch the tone of someone trying to explain the miracle of lights coming on in twilight, in afternoon, with their sense of ready anticipation. The speaker uses technicalities of evolution and bureau of power, and then catches up the more amazing technicality of eyesight developing toward the need to see. I guess the poem couldn't be rambling. The lines are closely held by stresses which keep turning out, against odds, to be five, and finally become easily and conclusively regular in the idea toward which the lines move.

"For Futures" was printed in *Lines at Intersection*, 1939, my first book (it was easier to get published in those days), and I think those poems were trying to hold close to instants of understanding for which I'd now try to allow more time and relaxed participation.

— J.M.

ROBERT PENN WARREN

The Return: An Elegy

The east wind finds the gap bringing rain:
Rain in the pine wind shaking the stiff pine.
Beneath the wind the hollow gorges whine
The pines decline
Slow film of rain creeps down the loam again
Where the blind and nameless bones recline.

    they are conceded to the earth's absolute chemistry
    they burn like faggots in — of damp and dark — the monstrous
                bulging flame.
    calcium phosphate lust speculation faith treachery
    it walked upright with habitation and a name
    tell me its name

The pines, black, like combers plunge with spray
Lick the wind's unceasing keel
It is not long till day
The boughs like hairy swine in slaughter squeal
And lurch beneath the thunder's livid heel.
The pines, black, snore *what does the wind say?*

    tell me its name

I have a name: I am not blind.
Eyes, not blind, press to the Pullman pane
Survey the driving dark and silver taunt of rain.
What will I find
What will I find beyond the snoring pine?
O eyes locked blind in death's immaculate design
Shall fix their last distrust in mine

    give me the nickels off your eyes
    from your hands the violets
    let me bless your obsequies
    if you possessed conveniently enough three eyes
    then I could buy a pack of cigarettes

In gorges where the dead fox lies the fern
Will rankest loop the battened frond and fall
Above the bare tushed jaws that turn
Their insolence unto the gracious catafalque and pall.
It will be the season when milkweed blossoms burn.

the old bitch is dead
what have I said!
I have only said what the wind said
wind shakes a bell the hollow head

By dawn, the wind, the blown rain
Will cease their antique concitation.
It is the hour when old ladies cough and wake,
The chair, the table, take their form again
Earth begins the matinal exhalation

does my mother wake

Pines drip without motion
The hairy boughs no longer shake
Shaggy mist, crookbacked, ascends
Round hairy boughs the mist with shaggy fingers bends.
No wind: no rain:
Why do the steady pines complain?
Complain

the old fox is dead
what have I said

Locked in the roaring cubicle
Over the mountains through darkness hurled
I race the daylight's westward cycle
Across the groaning rooftree of the world.
The mist is furled.

a hundred years they took this road
the lank hunters then men hard-eyed with hope:

ox breath whitened the chill air: the goad
fell: here on the western slope
the hungry people the lost ones took their abode
here they took their stand:
alders bloomed on the road to the new land
here is the house the broken door the shed
the old fox is dead
The wheels hum hum
The wheels: I come I come
Whirl out of space through time O wheels
Pursue down backward time the ghostly parallels
Pursue past culvert cut fill embankment semaphore
Pursue down gleaming hours that are no more.
The pines, black, snore

   turn backward turn backward in your flight
   and make me a child again just for tonight
   good lord he's wet the bed come bring a light

What grief has the mind distilled?
The heart is unfulfilled
The hoarse pine stilled
I cannot pluck
Out of this land of pine and rock
Of the fallen pine cone
Of red bud their season not yet gone
If I could pluck
(In drouth the lizard will blink on the hot limestone)

   the old fox is dead
   what is said is said
   heaven rest the hoary head
   what have I said!
   . . . I have only said what the wind said
   honor thy father and mother in the days of thy youth
   for time uncoils like the cottonmouth

If I could pluck
Out of the dark that whirled

Over the hoarse pine over the rock
Out of the mist that furled
Could I stretch forth like God the hand and gather
For you my mother
If I could pluck
Against the dry essential of tomorrow
To lay upon the breast that gave me suck
Out of the dark the dark and swollen orchid of this sorrow.

❧ ☙

I have chosen this poem for two reasons — first, the peculiar circumstances of its composition, which has led to a good deal of mistaken supposition about it, and second, because it makes a point concerning a cliché that appears here and there about my early stages of work.

As for the first, I began to teach, at Southwestern College in Memphis in 1930, and went to Vanderbilt University at Nashville, in the fall of 1931, having spent the summer in California. While there, I found most of my serious life in reading or working at poetry. "The Return" is of that summer, the only poem of the season that I have preserved (I think). While there, I received a letter from my father saying that my mother was not well, but expressing no grave concern. When the letter arrived I was fumbling at a poem, or poems, continuing the "Kentucky Mountain Farm" group. (And here I may add that I had then never been in the Kentucky mountains — they simply provided a romantic spot in my imagination; in fact, I had never even seen, to my knowledge, a mountaineer, the first I was ever to know being Jesse Stuart, whom I came to know well when he was a student at Vanderbilt a couple of years later.)

I suppose that the suggestion of the situation of the poem may have, unconsciously, come from my father's first letter. But I took him at his word that there was no reason for apprehension. The poem was pure fiction, and a spin-off from the group mentioned. The poem is not specific about the geographical location of the "groaning rooftree of the world," but I had definitely in mind that the son was returning from the East (vaguely New York) and crossing the Appalachians to the western slope, as I had done on various occasions. The inset line "a hundred years they took this road" refers, of course, to the long migration beginning, say, with the "Long Hunters," who came to Kentucky. The "lost ones" are those who dropped off on the western slope, still in the mountains, on poor soil, isolated from the busy world.

The poem was finished, or nearly finished, before another letter told me that my mother was really ill, but that there was no reason for me to come back before the time I would begin at Vanderbilt (my home was only fifty miles from Nashville). Just as I was about to leave California, a letter reported that her illness had taken a turn for the worse. Stopping only to report the situation to Vanderbilt, I drove directly to my little home town over the Kentucky line, where a man I knew who happened to be on the street, told me that she was in a hospital in Hopkinsville (a larger Kentucky town some twenty odd miles away), and in a serious condition. I drove on — it was night now — to the hospital, in a state of great agitation, but certainly in no state resembling that of the fictional "I" of "The Return." But I do remember that the poem (in which I had felt, or hoped, that I had made some sort of break-through) seemed a thing of evil omen, tangled with all sorts of emotions and crazily with some sense of nameless complicity and guilt. (And now I hazard that this fact may have, unconsciously, prevented my pursuing this type of poem until years later.)

At the hospital I was not allowed to see my mother that night. So I joined my father in a silent vigil. Next morning I did see her, shortly before an operation. She lingered for a day or two, and the family and I watched her slowly sliding toward death. She was fully aware of everything, full of love for us, sporadically summoning strength enough to talk to us until almost the end, smiling at us when she was too tired to talk. She died on October 5, 1931. The mountains of my poem were far away, eastward, across the long Commonwealth of Kentucky.

More than thirty years later, I succeeded in writing a group of poems, really a longish poem, about her death, under the title "Tale of Time." It is not fiction.

My second point concerns the kind of poem "The Return" is, and its context. It is sometimes said that in my struggle up to "Billie Potts," the dominant influence was that of the Metaphysical Poets. This is simply not true. "The Return" is one among many poems in which there is no relation to that kind of poetry. It is a very "open" poem, much more the kind of poetry I have been writing in the past twenty-five years, somehow, despite the prevalence of rhyme, resembling in variety of line length, and structure, a kind of free verse. And then, of course, the contrapuntal insertions give an effect far different from the tight structure of "metaphysical" poetry. Actually, the influence of the "metaphysicals" is really shown in my second volume *(Eleven Poems on the Same Theme)* which includes work from the second half of the decade of the 1930's, though one poem, "The Garden," dates back to 1933 or 1934.

Besides "The Return," and the kind of poetry it represents, there were in that early phase several basic kinds of poetry far different from Donne *et al*, poems derived from balladry ("Pondy Woods," of the late middle twenties, one of several poems about the black world, which had a mysterious and poetic fascination for me, poems published but not collected), a number under the shadow of Hardy (who is still very important for me) or even direct imitations of him, as "The Garden" is a deliberate imitation of Marvell (poems published but not collected), and a number of poems of tightly structured stanzas, with rhyme, but not "metaphysical" in spirit or method ("To a Friend Parting" or "Late Subterfuge"), and certain poems of the early 1940's (such as "Terror," "Original Sin," and "Pursuit").

What I am getting at is simply this: up to the publication of my first *Selected Poems* (1943), I was reaching out in various directions, submitting myself, sometimes quite consciously, to various influences, experimenting (not so much with technique as with tone, feeling, spirit), fumbling to find a voice — or myself. I have here used "The Return" because it most dramatically illustrates my experiments and fumbling, with relation to earlier poems ("Kentucky Mountain Farm," and others), and because it somehow gave me a base for the future. For ten years after the first *Selected Poems*, I could not finish an ordinary shortish poem, though I did do one book-length poem, "Brother to Dragons" (1953). I have felt for a long time that the poetry that began again in 1954 was somehow indebted to "The Return" in a number of ways.

—R.P.W.

Part Two

FIVE POETS

I

The Motive for Dancing

Doug Abrams

Doug Abrams is a poet and a lawyer. Born in Greenville, South Carolina, he remained in the South, completing his undergraduate and law training at Wake Forest University. During these years he wrote hundreds of poems, his manuscripts seeming to come from an energy as unending as the life of plants, rivers, and marshes he wrote about. Studying textbooks by day and writing poems by night, Abrams quickly absorbed ideas and images. By the time he was twenty-one years old, he had had poems selected by the editor of *Poetry*, others following in *Wind, Chelsea, Descant,* and *En Passant.* He practices law in Raleigh, North Carolina. Doug dedicates *The Motive for Dancing* to the memory of his father.

The Marshes

I stand on the marshland where the
   waters burn through weeds
and light thickens into the worming haze of
cypress knees, and from the wood peaks of savannahs,
sea and light settle across the land.

All night coves fill and recede, birds
   drum in their trees, the brackish shores
reverse themselves, longing first for the sanddunes
and then being swamped into basins only to grow
coarse with regret and waffle back toward
the beach, like minnows shifting along ebb lines.

At morning I bring myself to walk the beach,
to see what's missing and if the tides have
   borne the darkness well or if gulls
and blackbirds will handle the sea's wind
like the pear leaves holding to their gallows.

The rivers have been herded
to the salt-water swamps,
their mountain-murk dense
from harsh rutted tides —

we may observe the last breed
of warblers
to manipulate the wild-cherry
shrubs or egrets to haul crabs
from these bogs.

But each night the water
eludes us,
skulking away until the dikes
lord over weeds
and we're left listening
to the basin's ebb.

Protection

These disasters I offer without recourse —
wind as it uproots slant-pines,
limbs distended over brittle weeds
as if contemplating their losses
or deferring to land's religious decaying.

Each storm bears its own regret;
winter only mockingbirds verge against snow,
but by another fall
leaves singe, descending like geese,
in a squall.

Nothing worth protecting survives —
when light zinnia blooms drift toward
recedes, it's dusk at bare minimum;
they attain different angles by morning;
my shortages are accumulating too;
I've scarcely touched the night
when it's flawed with sun, horizon
levelling the former darkness there.

There's a permanence to this dusk,
different from spring where yellow-maples
seem to outlast the darkness indefinitely,
& unlike early fall when newly lessened
oaks release the few leaves remaining.

In winter land's intangible,
mockingbirds lunge into hollows
without interfering with the terrain's
bleak consistencies.

Everybody lately has had shortages,
I'm no exception, though sorrow's
at an abundance high even by my standards —
I may be devoid of relatives
if things continue.

Our infirmities hunch
like crows in the yews,
a sort of humbling posture
similar to seedlings overlooking
gorges; their roots paw

at earth, though each added limb
may render its height unbearable;
why must I be hung
over cliffs, counting ledges,
measuring distances between them
& focusing on bottom-rocks?

For once I'd like to sight
the precipice & recognize hospitable
waters, pools with the assurance
of depth, the unmarred surfaces
denoting a river with sustaining flow.

Sympathy

I happened on the woodthrush,
dense as winter itself
with snowed boughs of dogwoods
inhospitable again — it'd expected
nothing of this sort, disoriented
as if alien to the climate.

The last bird I rescued
lasted a few hours,
a cedar waxwing which tracked
a monarch butterfly to our window
& veered into glass.

I'm inept at healing wings,
though I can detail
how external feathers
extend in their death-roll,
slight jerkings near the neck
as it contemplates flight
& nerves respond, crippled.

I would welcome the killing light
        which led me into a descent so vague
no sorrow could find me
            and there I would strip the stars
of their reticence;

nobody has returned from their graves,
        so it mustn't be any worse
than what they've left
            or a loophole would be located,
that's human nature;

I imagine a hole so profound
        no shadow escapes
and the sum of its walls are so complete
            in their darkness as the center

and I've been told how if I climb the
Empire State Building a floor at a time
        in my mind, I'll lose my misgivings;
there must be a similarity there

which connects the arc of our heights
        with the land we are soon part
of because the trees shake their branches
            down on the earth
while sending their leaves seeking sun;

it's a risk they have to take
        if they want to continue
and to know their limbs weighed with blossoms
        and the feel of water separating
them from weeds.

Tenet

I'm not philosophical; when oaks stray
across the gaps in wind
I don't compare their grief
to geese huddled on marshes
where tides sift through weeds
in unceasing indirections.

I don't expect light
to lunge from dusk boughs
though each morning leaves char
with sun; when I ford
rivers, I don't speculate
on water's flaws at rapids below,
beyond my sight, how blackbirds may traverse
the hollows as basins herd broken creeks
from cliffs.

There's nothing the wilderness
requires of me that light won't provide —
rousing frogs to their low despair,
or webbed in the willows
like grief itself.

They're cutting in my neighbor's heart
and adjusting its rhythms — it doesn't
keep the correct time and they want
it nearer the mysticism of stars,
to bear its own weight; it's like a river
in there, marshy bogs creating channels,
pines emerge to house blue-jays.

We know we're so near grief,
it could define us, kin from unhampered
cars which slow on the streets,
as if to address us, when they realize
they're intruding.

They had no problem with Grandma Ana,
the bay-sand dug nicely and though grass
won't keep, nobody I know minds;
afterwards, we closed the doors
on the porch, while dusk
birds shifted in the grey palms,
and tried to dance the walls down.

Chopping Block

The flow of the axe
must be as if light, a descent without
hesitation, the balancing of impacts
    across the planes of wood;
that is the separation of seasons,
I'm aiming for, to split across drought
where the tight spindles weigh the tree,
and to have the lush spring growth
cut through — the sapwood easier at that interface;

I learned about the direction of trees
one winter where lightning
    wrecked a yellow-maple and I wedged
kindling for a week of sleeting and thaw
as the sun lightened the poplars;
now it's winter, when I throw
the dull blade, as it is spring when
    we collect pineneedles for mulch;
our deeds as much as the reduction of trees,
indicating what month we're in;

the cedar waxwings rely on a different system —
as the dusks tow darkness up, so do they gauge
    their flight; you know where you are by elimination;
when the junipers show their berry-cones,
blackbirds appear, though no geese
are emerging from marshes.

Conveyance

As the clapboard rows
          reconcile
themselves to this evening,
rooms inhabited by lamps,
shadows edge across yews;

a couple reweeds their half-garden
of wrecked tulips,
and designs barriers of mulch;
what will those disjoint
stems, thin as blighted cedars,
uncover of the earth?

Will they unburden
themselves of an unspeakable
logic — in the shape of bulbs
abandoning dormancy
for a week's respite at spring?

Perhaps they surface
after winter as a reiteration
that nothing lasts,
even seasons,
or blossoms,
or the houses whose dens disperse
like hemlocks
discarding light.

Night Train

Moon is thick as a gourd beyond the willow
    row — it's one of those transitions
where one instant you're conversing
and the next a red light's poking through windows
    on the city's edge and no one speaks
    for fear their tongue won't work —
I've heard of innumerable relatives
departing in that fashion.

The train hasn't been bothered much
    from its rhythm,
etching across the hill leaves,
graceless as lame wheels lunge
for the correct rail.

Freight cars sound
as if they'll untie themselves,
wobbling loose like geese
and I let the darkness
    in my window, but it's sewn
to the wind in splotches.

My grievances, I realize, have gaps,
I can't cover every niche
of disaster;
and yesterday I parodied
myself at the local
high school, instructing
them on poetry's necessities,
while they speculated
on the 2nd shift,
which I recall from the mills
as the widows' shift;
and having gauged the looms'
wobble until that rhythm
stayed with me three months
into autumn,
I can't begrudge them
their indifference.

We've shared the heritage
of waters, laden
in the innumerable hulls,
& have retained corpses
in burlap for ballast;
it's not a constitutional,
acknowledging mockingbirds
shearing worms from milkweed;
it's no feckless jaunt
through backwoods, a diversionary
trek so as to emerge
rejuvenated.

Beyond this grief
there's a rationale
as meaty as a katydid shell;
it preys on us,
though we're conciliatory,
for the most part.

Things Are Rough All Over

The way rain flees these hills
I'm not astounded to hear
there's a reluctance in light, unearthed
from the poplars.

When I travel these streets
     I expect the worst,
swamp-like alleys where all afternoon
beggars assemble as numerous as house-sparrows
in maples.

One night rivers will decline
     to abide in marshy basins,
& cliffs will resist wind's scarring;
in the interim I edge rough corners
with my suspicions
in hand, trusting the wilderness
to heal itself.

Tonight we are lonely, the wind narrows
through streets like the weight of our grief,
which waggles like a snake through our rooms;
I'm not mourning the deaths this hour
when the rain's miserable in its ragged
clothings. It's as sorry as we are,
dissolute, without parallel so low is it
reaching for.

And the dreary avenues limp toward
a square because they have no place to go,
because the rain follows the gullies that way.
We can hear the rain leaving, disturbing
the slick leaves, but we don't rush to
our windows. It will rain again and

though the corpses may not still
poke through the bright chips of water,
carrying the glow of torches through the
streets of Damascus, there are sorrows
enough to keep us occupied and needing
the rains.

I can't slow the train as I take myself
in sleep to Baltimore, my old body
fitting the bed above my brother
and we will visit my great-grandmother
in her ninety-ninth year as she whispers
yiddish to my grandfather, both of whom

are now speechless in the ground of my
memory; I must lose this dream myself
when my own groundworks call and
will face that calm in whispers; I will
listen to the wheels as they finally
ease into flight, into the skies I
believed my father's mother lived on when
he flew to visit her; what do I have to
give my children as I give up with my
body and place it dead on the sheets?

I will tell them of my wife as we
drove to be married, I think, and the
sight of my mother as her treeline broke
into seedlings; I will hold myself to their
judgment, as to hers then, and will break
at last.

There's a reduction
in the cities,
not noticeable,
and it doesn't stall
traffic; but widows
gauge it at night
when moon consumes their attics
or a distant train
hesitates at crossings;

I'm amenable to their grief,
nothing less than solitude
will fit me,
as quail straggle
to intractable thickets
or Bachman Warblers
won't couple unless so homed
in the wilderness
man doesn't taint them.

Each night we're named,
families recede
at their fringes,
like water shucking waste
wake until lighting
on shores
& then on reentry
more excess burls
along sand;
nobody can rectify
the redemption to them,
but still the line extends,
irrevocable.

The fig tree has hung the wind
          from its branches and harbored
     its fruit; and the tree is neither
     one nor the other but
          the sum of both as the final rock
joins the mountain to outreaching sky;

     that is the highest union
          which brings the tree to bear
     or the mountain to its altitude;
          that is the building upon
which two can find a house and open the
     walls like a fig blooming and making
     life of winter;
and the scarce light is twined
          until it flows into the blossoms
     and the empty limbs
                    weigh with fullness;

and where two like a river
          are forged from the small
                    directions of creeks
     as one, there is a rock
     to be built upon,
          a foundation no wind disturbs.

Shepherds are defunct,
in Russia when wind verges across saplings
there's no predicting how many severed
leaves contain my heritage —
my great-grandfather lit like a moth
against the elm, his servant's knife wedged
between his lungs.

I turn their grief in my hands
and it doesn't weigh much —
distant as the listless dispersals
of foliage amid coverts
& backwoods I've never visited.

Tonight stars are intractable,
though moon-glint suspended under birches;
& I can't forecast how many squalls
they've in store or if in another winter
I'll collect their shorn branches
among jayweed.

Complaints

41

Even the flat-headed sparrows
avoid me, hostile to any part of this shaggy
hull — a split and untenable
shadow to the reckoning of their eyes —
who am I in my own weak sight,
    the light I obstruct or lines
wobbling on walls as I shift
from one nonplace to another?
    I'm the singular authority on mediocrity,
even my average's average,

I make a crowd by myself — this is a talent;
if I were a hermit, possums
wouldn't sidle up to me;
I'm the seeds of my own darkness,
    where I traverse, nothing good
follows; I hold the simple willows
and they're diseased, thinnish
leaves drowning in the waters;
when I speculate on stars,
    they implode, awkward
as eider ducks engaged over brackish marshes.

It would plague his bones to
bring himself into the woods and the open
seasons, opened to the eye, but without
speech, in the drizzle of cones in the slight
winds, hickory nuts splintering their
soggy walls; he would have taken

anything to be done with himself in that place
where the world remaining after a rapid jig
or swoon night would bear
weight upon him; he could not
think of a less desirable life than
that imposed by his deft tongue and his
religious postures against the stars,
their whooping light through the crowded
spaces; and he much preferred those

grand highways and ordered grassbacks
to raise his thoughts to the common
plots of the daily straits, the narrow
surfaces swift as a pond without the
sea's trying tides, but he knew his residence —
fields of softwoods throwing around their
seeds to the air, running cedars blazing
along the top soil; this was his world
and he couldn't escape to or from it,
but as a horn-rimmed owl would neither
take the night in exactly or be calmed
in the straight day's heat.

He ordained himself the man who would
not speak, and clearly he was so,
and climbed deep into the lush elm
and rested there until his bones sank
into the earth and were no longer rattled
by his thinking.

II

The Last Striptease

Barbara Friend

Barbara Friend gardens, runs, and occasionally tapdances "to keep sane." These diversions she balances against the demands of work in the admissions office at Colgate University, acting, studying for a Master's degree in Counseling, and writing poetry. Participation in workshops, among them Bread Loaf, helped her to concentrate her interests on poetry. She has published in *Poetry Northwest, Yankee, The Virginia Quarterly Review, The Poetry Society of Georgia Yearbook,* and *The Smith.* Among her awards is the Gassner Prize in 1976 from the Poetry Society of America. Born in Easton, Pennsylvania, educated at the University of Washington at Seattle and at Colgate, Friend lives with her husband and two children in Hamilton, New York.

Bushkill Park

I am bored
by this jackass
stapled to the floor.

I want a horse
that eats hills, flying
on a stalk of brass

my heart overhead
tugging on its string
candy apple red.

I must have a man
with a wing moustache
taking tickets at a run

mirrors to wear
me sixteen startled ways
a calliope blaring

The Skater's Waltz.
When the wooden arm swings
into a gargoyle

I'll snatch ten rings
from its nose, stack them
on my thumb, never fling

them back, just whistle
home scuffing gum wrappers
past the nickel

a throw, destiny
clanking in my dungarees
like found money.

For Eve

Eden was edited, of course
cropped to exclude
this rife spread of orchard.
Saplings recede
in no defensible order

toward the vanishing point
like mushroom clouds. Knowledge
was here from the start
ambiguity coiled in the sedge
of the strictest heart.

Folly is never singular
which later we call Sin. Observe
how the groundlings scrabble for
windfall like good wives
at a white sale. One pair defers

for the weal of the State.
Some pious burghers of Heaven
swap morals at the garden gate.
God's in the money again
and all's right.

Adam's Rib

Jennifer Kaiser
class of fifty-eight
taught 11th grade Chaucer

and had more bones
than a saint. Spare parts
labeled one to nine

plus an odd clavicle
thrusting through her blouse
one April.   Ritual

internes clustered
to watch the surgeon pull
weeds, and plaster

her in like snowfall.
She was always under siege
wore bad times in gold

chattering at her wrist.
Tonight a stunned year convalesces
and I wonder where she is.

Hey Jenny, do they still
spade up each summer's
prolific burial?

And what about the bones
which must be of some use
in a Philistine time.

Her Old Man

He is brown
at the edges
and seems to keep

legends between
the cotton in his ears.
A gold chameleon

pins his fedora down.
Under splayed feet
dangling sits a fat

beagle, muzzling
cold toast
from his bleached hand.

When he twists
off the counter stool
a tweed penguin

rocks out the door.
She sees him go.
How can he still be there

jack-in-the-box
in his Punchy nose
and wool stocking cap

ready to bark
when she opens her
mouth, crouching

inside her forever
on his snake
of legs?

She looks into this candid day
and reads no sigh.
She does not hear snow

stop the cry of corners
or see the penitent hill
pose for its mask of death.

Her gauzy breath
asks nothing of the air.
Chill worships her.

A mawkish child
she will not learn reflection
believing the tufted sky

the candied trees
to be just what they seem.
God knows I've tried.

Her hour will come
bell, book and candle
swimming up like apples

in a slot machine.
For now my charms are tied.
She scars my counterpane

skimming the lovesick ice
needing no glass to claim
that she is beautiful.

It is the ironic death
obliquely caught
that will do me in.
The grade B movie queen
beheaded in casual prose
on a back page of the Times.

The farm wife struck
by lightning on Labor Day.
Her children still watch
a picnic hamper burn
in the rearview mirror
of their father's pickup truck.

Tonight, a girl's name
frailer than bird shell
will fall through my mind.
Has fallen from the mezzanine
of North Station, Boston.
Is falling head first
thirty odd feet
to the sudden concrete floor.

My unmet daughter
pinioned at twenty-three
for you I pull on once again
my threadbare cloak of humanity
while Sunday morning offers up
its routine casualties.

He is risen, I am told,
to hang like a hawk
in the bruised April sun
over this year's tithe of animals
splattered on the road.
For us pale unbelievers
you have only begun to fall.

Lullaby

You ask me body and I sing you bone
light as a whim, chalking its supple dance
on a dark time, chiding the printed stone
to speak in sudden tongues of innocence.

You ask me body and I sing you flesh
moon flower folded at the stoop of night
taking the simple now, tasting no wish
for ripeness of the spirit's appetite.

You ask me body and I sing you blood
strange exultation at the door of birth
casting my song adrift upon the flood
painting new seasons for a wasted earth.

But oh my children, not the subtle tune
that I would lose and you will find too soon.

Each morning at eight
he takes out the children
from a slot in his vest
checks the date
in their pert china faces
and inflates them
with a small bicycle pump.
They rise like soda pop
heads cropped at the ceiling
their stretched and printed smiles
advertisements for himself.

Coffee, a danish
and the early news.

Pulls out his wallet
and pinches the sides
of a plastic window.
Its mouth slits open
like a snapdragon
and he removes his wife.
Unfolds her, a wise saying
clipped long ago from the paper
and flattens her with his thumb.
Reads her like a fortune cookie
and slides her under
one corner of the blotter.
A jaundiced eye stares up.

Whiskey neat
and biscuits at three.

Reels in the children
unbuttons their tails
eases the life out of them
and tucks them back
into their worsted sleep.

Pleats the wife
in her accustomed places.
She is a perfect triangle
an American flag
pressed like a moth
into her dream of celluloid.

Elegy for a Lobsterman

You'd never blow
even when the traps came up dry
time and again, every
cleat line cut or bait rig snatched
even when the warden once
dropped anchor on your toe.
Words were as scarce
as moon snails in the catch.

Now when I cast back
fist over hand to haul scenes up
from summer's mildewed floor
it is your John Deere cap
that shades my eyes
your six league boots that clap
at my tall story thighs.

Guttering Irish moss
the trap breaks water, rank
dungeon for rock crabs, barnacles
and you: all jagged carapace
at eighty-four, queer throwback
to staunch Yankee stock
freckled pincers snapping

at foul winds, union buzzards
and the cost of twine
hungers larger than legal size.
I toss you clear, minding
how they never found body, boat
or gear, and set about mending
my net. Fergus, you're one
the poachers will never get.

A word begins.
Syllables thicken
inside their paper caul.

If I remain quite still
a single thought
will heave into light
under broad quill
and before pâté.

At the moment
of least assent
meaning will yellow forth
each celibate oval
slowly giving place
to the next.

On fresh linen
clarities
will be deposited
gleaming.
A legacy of glitter.

The sun is ice.
This dumb wait fattens
my August greed
and Chicken Little cries.

The black hood
settles on my beak.
The crisp axe
sings at my downy side.

I've lived so long
in voices not my own
I can't be sure
these words are mine.

I've left the theatre
to maunder home
not caring
that each zombie nerve
was pilfered from the dark
I put behind.

I've slipped myself
with expert deftness
into the hearts of friends
to outfox enemies
certain my time would come.

Last night
I thought it had.
Today I shy from edges.
Plummet I'd break
but unlike sponges
not regenerate.

Instead
my brittle shards
would each rise up
mocking the shape
of other lives now dead
to flee and leave me
uninhabited.

For what it's worth
I am waiting
for a shower of gold.
Not the debased sexual
coin of Danae's god
but a rash guttering of the stuff
my sugarfree daddy said
doesn't grow on trees.

Virtue is down two points.
Ambition leads in the stretch
but where's the percentage?

When the monsoon came
Midas corroded at the sight
of every gilt edge poppy
gone to seed, and forgot
that the best things in life
are compounded quarterly.

Not me.
I'm ready any time
to ride a heathen calf
through the starting gate.
If Aphrodite's wealth
dropped at my feet
I'd grab the apples and win
flaunting my nouveau richesse
like a Sunday school pin
for perfect attendance
at making do.

Read me no rhyme
of probability. Ods
bodkins, Love, unreason
is my middle name.

In a thicket
of lottery stubs
I am waiting for rain.

Cartography

The veins
of my left wrist
are green. You travel
them till they vanish

in the blind foothills
beyond which that masked
bandit, my heart,
calibrates its booty

like Ali Baba.
Who said anything
about love? I am wary
of heights, and you

of distances. We
are simply coordinates
that happened to meet
at a point

overlooking the old city.
You held me up to the light.
I came suddenly clear
a boy's treasure

map etched in code
warmed over candle
flame till the edges curl.
Skittish now

you inch down the grade
where a forester unsnarls
his skein of wood
and wild squirrels

turn to stone. Your hands will stay

on my back
like a day in the sun.

Last Will

Peas are late.
He cups each pod
like a prayer.
Ten year old
hands of ancient
batik move faster
than lizard tongue.

He runs
a blunt fingernail
down one green cocoon
counts a rosary within.
With snap of thumb
fires three pips
at a migrant worm.

No smack
from the old man
dead on his knees
near El Paso.
They planted the locust
brown husk of him
for next year's harvest.

Sun quits the furrow.
Last shells plock
into their slatted box.
Under unpicked stars
Juan burrows
into his father's skin
and sleeps.

The runner leaves
her shoes at the door
to fill with snow

as if
the blinding silks
were enough

as if
the black tea
poured into cinnabar cups
were enough

or the lacquered
syllables that pass
like angelfish
through the fabulous
screen

while
the nub of her
waits intact
at the center

who slept
with the white leopard
desert nights
dreaming the unbinding
beyond feet.

The Last Striptease

for my mother

After the sequins
cool, and even
the censor's ink

pasties drop
like tarnished pennies
to the runway

she pauses, dressed
in the choice
graffiti

of her skin. Zip
without warning
she slips

off her guard
steps out of her guilt
exhibits every scar

and zip
she is grinning
straight from the hip

easy
in the audacity
of lust, and the stage

is littered
with disbelief. Awkward
in the sudden light

of silence
she is learning
to put on her clothes.

High Time, Too

Am shucking
the life that knows
too well, how
it is faring.

Have always
started out deep
to wind up
shallow.

Now enter
the picketed
fin-black
water

no bearing
but skin, blanched
as the under
bark of birches.

III

The Bridegroom
of Mytilini

Maria Ingram

Maria Ingram was born in rural North Carolina where she rode the backs of tobacco sleds and refused to learn the multiplication tables. After so much water, so many bridges, she has created a unique food shop in Winston-Salem where she is called upon to know such things as how much six and a half ounces of Brie @ $3.85 per pound is, which is only justice. Her studies at the University of North Carolina at Chapel Hill and Pfeiffer College did nothing to teach her multiplication, but she learned the mysteries of poetry. In pursuit of what she did know, she has written poems and taught in North Carolina in the Poetry in the Schools program. Her work has been published in *Beloit Poetry Journal*, *Red Clay Reader*, *Southern Poetry Review*, *Carolina Quarterly*, *Foxfire*, and other journals. In 1976 *Maria*, a chapbook of poems, was published by Red Clay Books. When last seen, Ingram was counting on her fingers.

Wherever I go
the ghost of home goes.
Sometimes we have a
high old time of it,
whirling until the sun
pops out of western boxes
and we toast the incidental
rise with a goblet of
water from elysian wells.

Then there is Mycenae,
ominous,
blood in the tobacco rows,
birds swooping to pick
the scuppernongs of eyes,
a willow switch to bare
thighs in North Carolina
and the curdling screech of shame.

Other places more beautiful, less grim.
We watch sailors drop anchor with
machine gun rattle of
chain links, whooping like
cranes, flapping to shore.

Places where palms dip and
joy beads on the brain like honey.

But we always return to Mycenae,
as if flogged there.
It is the slaughtering yard from
which we can recognize sunrises in
their proper easts.
It is the uneasy harbor for which
we cannot but set sail.

The Indian poet, charting
territory, said a pale woman
could not know wolves

But my wolves sang to me at night
when I was under quilt and
the fireplace licked the ceiling
with tongues of light.

Winters later the kerosene stove
doilied the same ceiling.
The house was drunk with fuel;
its breath shamed my hair.
Still the wolves circled and sang.

First thing I remember on this earth
was a picture on the wall of a wolf
howling over a slain
or asleep
lamb in the snow.
Because I did not know the lamb
I could not know the wolf.

Do not, still.
In the caesura of hard winter
ice-dogged limbs crack through silences.
I lift; the scent is heavy with animal.

And I suspect he is always outside
these walls, suckling wild on
the raw teats of fear.
It is my not knowing
lets him sing
and me.

Aunt Ola of Abbeville, South Carolina

Aunt Ola, old,
sweet prize, every five
minutes stepped on her
porch to look through cataracts for
our car loaded with nieces of
her dead husband John
careening from five hours
of driving through mudholes
in backyards, off-course.

She gave us stories,
overhead light,
four beds of borrowed quilts,
damson jelly and talcum powder,
a sack of pecans she stooped to
pick from her spitting tree;
anything she could find,
she gave.

We drove off, leaving her
by the camellia bush
waving
waving until she was
a heatbeam
in her cold polyester dress
with the Sunday collar.
We knew we would never see her again.

She had said I love your bones.

She must have taken the bothersome
shade from the lightbulb she kept
banging into
and sat for a time,
hearing one ungiveable pecan drop
on her tin roof and another,
and at night the gunshot
when the trees bloom with wind.

Bad storms in August is why
I perch here on this stool and
swat flies while my mama cans peaches.
I do not belong here.
I know the alphabet of the owl
when he comes from nowhere into
the night to spell his name.

I know what a fish mouths when he
surfaces,
feel in my skin the darkling rising
of his going down.

I watch my mama move among the pans,
playing their drums to a roof-rain music
she cannot get the rhythm of, else
she would unlock the screen for me,
say shoo, bad little storm, fly
to that high-pitched whistle I
reckon you hear.

She pours into jars an amber thick
as voodoo, ugly with cinnamon.
Knowing she can save peaches by
releasing them to dark magics
what business does she think
I have swatting flies
and does it occur to her the
why of flies,
the ripe they're after.

The New Gordian Knot

The Church is ablaze with
golden ikons and gilt letters
that stand for light.
Having touched my candles to the fire
and kissed the mock feet of a
pinewood Jesus,
I sit on the women's side and
study the saints in
their expensive pictures.

To the hitching post
such a wagon as Gordus drove
into Phrygia is leashed.

My own Sotiris had said you
will come to unravel the Greeks,
but never, such a neophyte to war,
will they understand you.

In a fog of myrrh and mind, I try.
Is this the same carpenter I knew
in Sunday School oceans away?
He would have nothing to do with
perfume or kisses on picture frames.
This foreign Christ comes to an
indomitable people and proclaims
the sword is peace.
Mine snapped weapons in two like
kindling with kindness.

Tomb-cold sanctuary
the only music metallic echoes
of clicking heels and clinking coins,
not the womb of mine,
nor the sopranos.
A land bought with more
blood that I can fathom

has no sopranos.

At the Bridge of Alamana
where the pruned branches of
bodies littered the fair
garden of Greece,
Diakos was skewered like
a lamb to parade in the tall
grasses spiked with cyclamen.

Molon Laveh! Leonidas had shouted
to the ten thousand as he stood at
the bottleneck of Thermopylae with
his three hundred Spartans.
Holding his spear high,
its point winking in the sun,
Molon Laveh! Come and take it!
A massacre costlier
than the Persians dreamed.

Somewhere in stone I have read
      Arise the three hundred
      And see how like to you
      Your children are

But it is the children who arise.
Again and again they arise,
the handfuls,
the three hundreds against the
tens of thousands to claim
their home where once the
deep-throated Orpheus charmed
from the Sirens their song.

Oh Sotiri, my Greek,
my love,
you have led me to this altar
where I kneel

the stranger I will always be
to go about unplaiting
the cord in my way.
Alexander the Great slashed it
with his sword.
I worry the silence
for the first pick of fleece:
the hard honed steel
in a pin of radiant,
unaccustomed light.

But the mind, finally,
can only catpaw at
viperous edges.
To finger the sacred core
takes the heart.

I have worked like a plow mule my life.
There is some sweet Canaan, all I know.
Golden bayou, chili pepper sauce.
I'll be among that number sure as
I beat hell out of these keys —
Luden's cough drops on the tenor,
pocketbook in my lap,
gonna lay my burdens down, let em be.

It won't be for the shirts I've starched
nor for the floors I've scoured,
they don't amount.
They'll just say SWEET EMMA — they'll
have to make em step back a ways, let me pass.
They'll be wantin me to sing and I'll sing.
They won't say it's pretty, Lord they
know it's not pretty.
But they'll be apt to say give that
woman a catfish, let her be.

And I'll just traipse in my petticoat,
not hittin a lick.
If I know Jesus and his daddy —
and like middle C I do —
they will arrange to have a piano.

An Elm in Carolina

The widow wakes when something
worries the pane: sprinkling,
until rain turns moth and she opens
the glass to let the dreamer at the moon.
There is the elm, grand and dying in
a lunar pool, the swing somebody
grand and dead swung from
a limb by a strong rope.

The rope has been shortened year by
year from the bottom hitches as
legs have come to leap with
antelope precision by
the lion in the magnolia.

This is not a birch in the north woods
a young poet used to catapult to heaven on,
nor the cradling covenant that eased him down.
This swing swings more like a pendulum of
metered breaths where death is as
likely to come as a moth at the window.

The sailor, in the swell and fall,
remembers pretty Sophia who sells
popcorn at the movies.
He imagines her ironing blouses
in the moonlight by a pot of basil,
sprinkling the dry cotton with
water in a Coca Cola bottle
diked by her thumb,
humming, and seining the
sea for the Pericles.

One day she will come, he wishes,
her dark eyes red, her hair tossed
like a squall, and say take me, Vassili,
I am dead without you
and he will sail away on the cobalt waters
with a story to pull from his pocket
like a whittling knife.

If ever you get to the Odysseus Theatre,
he will say, his
sleeves rolled up like doughnuts,
stop by the little minaret of popping
corn and see if there is not a
wilting girl in a
starched white blouse
like a petal torn.

Bad blooded and exiled
the Indian just after
night snuffed out the sun
sauntered by the house on
a mule to feed a note in
the winesap and to go on to
wherever it was he made out he went.

My mother
before she was
would sail across the yard
to fetch the pulp
with its cidery sins
branding her hands—
"My swethart Marie—"

Her father would suspect
what business has that boy
with whiskey for blood
on this road every night.
My mother would examine
the scab on her elbow,
wishing dark angels.

The Indian would hit
yellow jackets one Spring
on his tractor at
a bad place in the field.
They were to rise up like
an anthem and leave him
the only good Indian
in the buttery nuggets of clay.

Bees bees bees
my mother would keen into
soughing trees
to make sure no one was listening.

I hear her say bees
when there are no pines
to sweep the word away.

But he was sorry as gully dirt, she says.
I didn't love him so much as
I ached for a dream I could not tag.
There were always games of
snap and tap and tag and,
truth be known,
I was pretty good.

On Earth's Sill, Before Entering

From the goat shed to the house
is a short journey by light of
the faintest star but the lantern
and all the lanterns lent
by heaven went out.

Hecate, Goddess of the Dark of the
Moon on nights when even the whites
of houses are silenced in black
prowls among the flowers.
I grope with the compass of
memory spinning wild.

My eyes wide as the eyes of poor
Oedipus, I wander the horrible yard
for a spark until I fear my own feet,
the rivers they will shepherd me into,
the abyss the ancients bore, the honied
net they laid for the wings of me.

I yield then to the dreaded
specter coiling in the bush.
What I remember flies from me like
a soul from the mouth of the dead
until its flutter is faint and
lost as I am lost.

And I am one with the darkness
that cloaks me, creamy and maternal.
From somewhere, a pulse, and
the wondrous, steaming night.
The lilac screams.
The young lambs nuzzle the straw.
The sun is mine, raging from this birth,
in the belly of a truer north.

Sunday afternoon we're sitting
in the backyard spitting seeds out
of bought watermelons and my
father says it's the worst
summer since 1930 when they had to
replant tobacco four times,
on into July, before it took hold.
Six and a half acres brought
a hundred and forty two dollars
at six cents a pound.
But there were some, he said,
only bought a half, a quarter
cent a pound.
One old man from Stokes County
crated up a bunch of chickens
to bring with him.
The auctioneer's fee was more
than his tobacco brought,
so he took his chicken money
to get back out into sunlight.
They sat around the camp,
laughing to keep from not laughing
at the fine mess they were in:
young'uns needed saddle oxfords
and notebook paper.
Daddy asked the man from Stokes
was he going to raise tobacco next year.
Oh yeh, he said, that's the only
thing they's any money in.

Outside Karditsa

The old man claims he can
mount the mountain in five minutes
with his seventy-five year old legs.
It is true.

She squats on the kitchen floor
to pluck feathers from a chicken.
He is racing up the mountain
she is plucking feathers
and night with dark talons
lights upon the earth.

The percolating bells of sheep
round the hill, white now
by a cloud of clouds on foot.
The shepherd stops at the gate
to say how fine the fig trees
look this year.

We build a fire with lemon wood,
cook the chicken, dish up
the yoghurt, wash the scallions,
pour the wine.

What Argo,
what ship is this that carries us
through the incubating dark as family,
what hand pours the oil of music
upon my head
and makes me call this old land home.

Whether for the first or
fortieth time
from the Acropolis
look over bleached, sad Athens
to the flowering corpses,
poppies the crimson of blood.
Shoulder the brooding sun like
a cross, stoop to loosen
your sandal in flesh as
Attika's Nike did in stone
and feel the thirst,
the quick of the insatiable
heart that rises on colt legs
to stumble for new pastures
and the pastel fans of mimosas,
the glacial pain of water.
It is the kindest mercy that
we do not die but what
we are born a thousand times.

Out of the Aegean a silver moon rises.
The women of Mythimnos sit on the cool steps
that soar to the acropolis like a falcon and
drop like a tern to the sea.
They have bought shiny eggplants by day and
have laughed the high gold-toothed falsettos;
they drone now, copper-colored, by night.

The talk is of Apostolis, who is to wed next
Sunday the ripest of all the village,
the fair Alexandra.

The bride is home rehearsing obedience
while Apostolis is at the tavernas only
Apostolis is not at the tavernas.
The tourist woman knows.
She lies with him and hears love
pounding in his dark chest like an exile.

> He is getting married next Sunday as you know.
> He has pointed to the darkness where I have
> met him night after night.
> Sometimes the darkness has been in streets
> where animals have congregated and
> I have delivered myself to their claiming eyes,
> sometimes on the perfumed reefs of flowerbeds
> or in the foothills under olives
> but most of the time it has been on the rocky beaches
> of Lesbos, love-haunted by that woman whose sandalfooted
> skipping I have heard when he has been asleep.
> I have cocked the shell of her songs to my ear
> and have heard the dirge of my own guarded heart.
>
> I have memorized him with my hands as he slept.
> I have toyed with the beer key he hangs
> around his neck for it is his job, opening beers.
> It says Hellas II and I can figure out the Hellas part

but I do not know the II and there is no way to ask
him for the only English he knows is french fries.

Besides, in this sweet death of sleep he is mine.
The sea laps its tympany tongues
and keeps watch with the dead woman's songs
and me.

But the rock grows granite and the moon is steel.
The wind has tired of its zephyrs.
I hear sandals flee down the sand until
I cannot hear anything but cold.
Into this forbidden place where earth
has fermented with the yeast of Aphrodite
I have sportingly reached and, cold,
white hungry cold, have
found this I cannot call the name of.

Anyway I finally shook him, I said I'm cold
Apollonius or whatever his name was
and he must have understood.

Maybe the tourist woman could be
a woman of Mythimnos,
could live for the passion,
bargain for the eggplants,
embroider her life in the long
stitches of afternoon on the steps.

Or maybe the island man could pack
his white shirts, turn from
the fallen gates of Priam and
board the bus to the plane to the
factories of the new world.

But the sea will have nothing to do
with a swallow;
and the sky will not honor a carp.

Once, beneath the moving acacias,
I watched him eat soup.
I was hiding behind poker for
seashells with an Englishman who
was prattling on about the destitute
lives of locals and asking
how come we couldn't have a go at
a meaningful relationship: something
cerebral and civilized and
altogether proper.

I was looking at flesh, sinews
hewn from Agamemnon, was seeing arms
draw soup to lips, the white bones of
fish stripped, the bestial snatches
of bread.
I had seen men eat like this before.

He had thrown his white servile shirt
a skin away, sat down to the bowl,
circling it with his arms, as peasants do,
guarding, for everything is thieving,
the very sun is thieving.

I heard the wind through the great
trees rise like surf.
Every full house was vacant; every
muscle a flush.
From the pink mouth of a shell
the wind claimed me for a tree.

Another time he dived into the water
to meet me where I stood.
He jetted below, wrapped my legs with
the tentacles of his arms and came up,
spraying like a porpoise, yards away.
I turned into the depths and
begged stranger arms to cradle me.

Oh having just risen from the bloom,
to be plucked then!
I was full of sweet life like a honeybee
whose legs are so heavy he can just
make it over the trees.
But he called to me.
In front of village eyes he called to me
my name, an infant word
I would need to live to answer to.

On the eve of the wedding day
when the village was choked with guests
and goats were preened with gardenias,
the island men answered their bodies
to the call of dance.
Apostolis slept with the tourist woman
on the beach.
From his chest he took the beer key
on its string and hung it around
her neck like a ruby which
is how the sun rose.

Apostolis flogged its thieving light
with stones.
He threw shells at the white cocks
crowing and wept.
Then he went to get a haircut
and got married.

The driver threw my suitcase on top of the bus.
I looked in every street and doorway for
Apollonarius or whatever his name was,
to touch one last time the bewildered eyes,
but the bus sputtered off down
the aisle of cypress in the sorrow,
ploughing new dust from the
old road Helen fled with Paris upon,
and I could not see anymore.

IV

Provocation

Kate Jennings

Kate Jennings has moved from New York to Virginia to Geneva, Switzerland, where she now lives with her husband and two children. She was born in Brooklyn, grew up in Richmond, was educated at Emory & Henry College in Virginia and Marymount College in New York, and has settled down a long way from home. But the themes, the settings, and the characters of her widely published poetry and fiction are rooted in America. She has had poems published in *The American Scholar, The Atlantic Monthly, Carleton Miscellany, Carolina Quarterly, Commonweal, The New Republic, Poetry,* and other journals. In 1976 some of her poems were included in a chapbook, *Second Sight,* hand-set by Robert Denham at Iron Mountain Press. One of her poems appeared in the Borestone Mountain *Best Poems of 1976.* Whether in America or Europe, Kate Jennings is at home in her language.

1

Our elf, malevolent gargoyle,
brews corrosive water, craft's fruit,
bitter and metallic: moonshine

forced through copper tubing under
branches webbed against a sky veined
with brass green light: moonlight

fanned on cornmash, kettle, oak fire,
outlaw squinting against heat, ash,
smoke, the chemist freezing at sight of

2

sheriff, skeet shooter, skilled stalker
armed with a long gleam, a slender
rod stocked with hot shot: a sly lump

of granite who'd walk on water: who
stalks through leaves leached to mold
and, heavy-handed, jams himself into

a crammed landscape where he scatters
shot, shatters silence, spills tinned
mulled white water: lightning. Now:

3

love like lust chars or seasons green
wood, sweetens wormwood. Sears stones
to powder: dust of lime, brim, moon.

Greed like love shines and gleams, stuffs
coal with silver, stops holes with wax
and waits. Waits. Heat releases: freed,

lust like greed shoots a straight shimmer:
freezes to quicksilver: metal, mercury.
Changes new brass for old. Dross to gold.

The tips of the maple's leaves turn
first, like sheets of paper that singe
around the edges before scorching
to burst up to flame: a burning bush.

The color crackles. But crackling fall
can't quite get off the ground. Keen days
will take over this lush heat, but not just yet.
It's a slow world. It turns slowly, easy-

going. Summer's final flush shades the full
fields, gilds the bumbling yellow jackets, clumsy
each morning with cold. The chill's burned off
by noon; then the plush green texture returns.

Hard not to wonder what witches do these days.
This must be their off-season. Soon cider, soon
scuppernong, squirrels hustling capped acorns,
soon frost on apples and pears; soon a ringed moon;

but meanwhile this richness, ripeness: do they
wander disconsolately, picking bristly chestnuts
for the sour pleasure of being pricked; kicking
fallen fruit with booted left-out feet, looking

ahead to September, October, November, to that
flowering bruised horned moon high-tailing it through
a bright sky at midnight, over a brown bleak earth
under cold stars, a world all lit up: a pumpkin,

glowing, a candle burning through eye holes and grin
and inside the sweep damp smell, sweet autumn, hectic
busy nights, sweet harvests, the damp flame scorching
the plump pumpkin's wet insides. Well, not just yet.

Lumbering along, slow and cumbersome as a honey-heavy
bear, fall drags her feet. Those covens must give up

sometimes, despair of her arrival, and just sit there,
scowling, arms folded, sullen creatures, their bony

backbones propping up tree trunks, their worn faces
grotesque as a sneer, embarrassment sketched like lust
on their features, scarlet in this heat. This hush.

The sunset's afterglow slants over the maples,
gilding stiffened grasses and stricken zinnias
and frozen purple pokeweed berries.

The chill deepens at dusk.
Leaves scuffle with a dry scrabble.
Underfoot the leaf-strewn path crackles.

Now the fox dines by moonlight on rabbits and mice,
relishing the fine-boned snap between his teeth,
moving his jaws dreamily over tender furred flesh.

Music warms them like lamplight:
chamber music: flutes, a violin.
The room's a cameo.

Beyond the onyx window
music ends and night begins
where something moves in the darkness,

a shape like a skeleton cat,
spine an arch,
fur fluorescent, striking sparks,

a bone cat on the prowl,
then, mangy, with needle teeth
and nine lives, maybe more.

A vicious hush, like held breath,
then the screech: the howl's
a scalding aural scratch,

a seizure of fury, seething grief,
pain, dropping scales and decibels
to a yowl, a long moan

that shudders the room's warmth,
a genuine shake-down.
The tentative flutes grate off.

A draft razors in across the floor,
chilling them and cooling the lamps,
filling the room with icy bloom,

and a child's timid knock
sounds like and resounds like
a fist on the door.

Garlic

The breath of life.

Aromatic and pungent, redolent
of the still nights all fall
when they swelled slowly under
ground, under the chill moon's
benevolent light: harvest,

they're braided into strips
and tied in bunches, potent crop,
to hang from the attic rafters,
dry, cold, safe from blight,
dangling next to the clumped onions
when the frost doilies the windows.

My knife slices the clove into wafers
to turn broth to stew, beast to meat.
The bud, a lumpy bulb,
would make a shapely pendant,
suspended on silver,
an elegant way to hold vampires at bay.

One clove in my fingers like a new moon:
economy itself, a conquest of space by taste,
sweet white and wrapped tight
in a purple skin, thin and innocent;
and a poem about garlic turns out to be

a poem about the moon.

I've thrown in this week's leavings: leftovers
spiced with spikes of peppercorns. I splash in
sherry to sweeten the pot, and lean close to see

what I've wrought. The watched pot boils;
I turn it down. A leek, sliced, surfaces,
floating next to a bobbing onion pierced

with cloves. The mixture I've concocted
bubbles up. My wooden spoon might be stirring
a stew brewed over live coals; this spoon

might be splitting the fat on broth brought
to a boil in spite of the huffs of windy weather:
were we gypsies, this stock would be stew.

As it is, the bay leaf bellies up to the carrot
over an electric coil. What I threw in
simmers sedately, ready to cool and freeze.

I stir cracked beef bones, add water and thyme,
and sit back to sniff at and smell the results:
spice, sherry, onions, carrots, turnips: stock.

Pisacano's window's a nightmare tangle
of seafood, shellfish, protein, energy:
squid, scungili, fish heads, soft shell
crabs, eels, cod, clams. Flawless bass
bedded on ice chips, their colors vein
vivid — muted purple, pure blue — lie
in perfect layers like nine dead cats.

Inside sawdust squeaks under my feet.
King crab chunks and lumps in tin cans
line the walls where the men are busy
and efficient, making fish bits fly
through the marine-scented air. Blood
splatters their white aprons as they
fillet the thin flounder. A lobster
flinches, then freezes under the knife,
his black and green shell stilled,
lichened tones stalled now in amber,
static, waiting for the boiling bath.

The oysters open with a chalky gritty
creak. In their bin the crabs rattle
and scrabble. I lift a limp pink shrimp
like a curled embryo, a headless curve
or line of raw crunch, scaled. Perch,
haddock, halibut, mackerel, snapper,
sole: fins, flippers, feelers, claws.

The Cook Dreams of Mushrooms

In the kitchen on the cutting
board under my knife or a still

life in the wicker basket slung
over my arm: something for nothing,

found clinging moistly to tree stumps
and trunks in dank places or rising

among roots: tough and creamy, smooth
flesh and rings of silky gills, smoky

brown caps bell-shaped (she turns in
her sleep, fingering the blanket,

and nearly wakes; her nap's uneasy),
stem bases bulbous, firm heads I can

almost taste (she licks her lips in
sleep and sleeps deeper), gathered

on autumn afternoons in air choked
with pollen dust and ragweed, motes

sparkling in sun shafts, stalks my
sticky hands curve around gingerly,

bits I fill my basket with, picking
buff or gray buttons to take home

and slice neatly and heat in hot
butter, tiny blotters puffing

in my burnished pans:
precious, luscious,

I could just
eat you up.

In the big field near the airport
two men are throwing mossy sticks
into the branches of the chestnut
to knock down the prickly fruit,

stamping on the husks to open them,
discussing fetishes as they stoop
to stuff the nuts into burlap sacks.
I'm leaning on the fence, listening

to the roar of a jet, thinking about
the strange weather lately, freak
storms and dry spells, the chaste
grey moon at dusk. The afternoon

is colorless, a woodcut of sky and
trees. A cat is walking through
the tall weeds, stalking to pounce,
then pausing, completely alert and

unmoving, and I'm watching him idly,
feeling itchy and needing to sneeze,
hearing snatches of talk behind me:
". . . or the sweet pains of celibacy."

The men drop their sticks at the root
of the tree and pick up their bags of
nuts and one gropes in his pocket and
tosses a catnip ball into the leaves

at their feet. The cat leaps to dart
after it, catches it in his forepaws
and turns three somersaults, forming
a circle of claws and fur, spinning.

Pastoral

for Teresa

When we walked up the little hill to take
the laundry from the line strung among
the pear trees, the grass was full of slugs.
Yellowjackets hollowed the rotten fruit
at our feet and two small snails clung
to a sheet, their shells a mellow brown.

Below us the men were roofing the new shed
with red tiles and the children were playing
with broken tiles in the dust. The two of us
bent stiffly, reaching into the clothes basket,
our big bellies hard as rocks. You were angry

and so tired. Up the road at the next house
the two farmers, Sunday hunters, shouted
and fired their rifles at the sky and you
started and murmured, "They must be drunk."

Woodsmoke in the air, indefinable as fear,
and us talking quietly, folding the dried
clothes on the hill above the house filled
with hungry men and tired children and flats
of vegetables molding and spoiling faster

than you could cook; and the reddened vines
on the stone walls, the tendrils stitching
the old stone, holding the wall together
around the orchard of pear trees, the pink
pears ripening and glittering, rich as
jewels in the ruddy late-afternoon sun.

That must have been the longest fall.
Tired, cold, hungry, angry, tense;
early dark, dense fog, apprehension,
money worries, insomnia, the smell
of a pumpkin rotting on the porch.

The desolation of those afternoons:
the deserted dorm, and me listlessly
leafing through the books on my desk,
trying to memorize the twelve tribes
of Israel for a test. Night sweats,

listening to the water pipes thumping,
the grating of tree branches scraping
the loose roof shingles. North wind
and cold rain, sour apples dropping
all night long. The dusty red velvet

curtains at the shuttered windows
and in the mornings the front walk
slippery with wet leaves. Windrows
of leaves shuddering in the wind,
the wind moving the shadows of trees

across the stone house wall, a glint
of light like gold catching my eye:
thin cold bright late afternoon autumn
sunlight on the dead vines clinging
to the brick wall in the back yard.

Years later, lying awake in another
country, surrounded by the deep sleep
breathing of my husband and children.
It's late, I'm tired, the house is
warm and quiet, why can't I sleep?

The steel sky's premature,
a grey rare for October. Over
our heads it's low and dense.

I said: *His eyes were clamped shut*
in timeless unearthly peace.

You backpack our living son. He pulls
your curls and shouts with laughter
to see the world from your height.

I said: *His eyes were shut tight.*

The three of us walk from stained glass
to tapestries, triptych to burnished sculpture,
mothers and sons, annunciations, births.

I said: *His eyes were shut, clamped shut.*

Now no one moves inside me,
now I nourish or neglect no one but myself.
The grey stones meet the sky without a seam.

I stand stock still, I freeze.
The gothic shapes raise my eyes.
I stand and stare around me, glazed,

the air gel-thick, hard to breathe,
no nourishment, nothing to do
but catch up with you two,

grab your sleeve, grin up at my son,
slow you both down and say
nothing. My lips clamped tight.

Breath and pulse are mere distractions.
Pain's pure, sheer, utter. Exquisite.
Its dumb throb drums and echoes
inside the poor numb skull.

The jaw takes on importance.
The jaw takes over, is more important
than that haywired mass, the brain,
that multi-celled pain-receiver.

The tooth must come out. Like a lover,
the patient weeps and aches to face such loss.
Then off to the dentist, where the jaw's rock.
The jaw locks in plain refusal

to admit the smocked doctor's instrument.
The shiny metal glitters, shooting sparks
that fizzle in the patient's crazed gaze.
The primitive reluctance to let him in gives way.

Crushed calcium shatters. The wisdom tooth
scatters under the hammer. A sliver, a shard
like a shark's tooth, a serpent's, sharp
white, leaves a hole, an obscene abscess

that thumps and bleeds no end. Spears
of light. Wads of bloodied gauze. Nauseated,
the patient feels his eyes glaze like aspic.
The hacked hole demands liquids, won't tolerate

a bite, not a fraction, of food. The vacuum
the gleaming tool caused and nature abhors
collapses slowly inward, and slowly heals.
Now nightly the patient dreams of extractions.

The moon's slower to bloom than to wane.
Fullness becomes her. Halved, she's abashed
and beats a hasty retreat, slinking off low
as though embarrassed by her own audacity.

In October she looks like an orange slice,
a piece of fruit left over from some summer
drink, wine soaked, stained, out of place
and sailing uncertainly through a dark sky,
tangled in tree branches like sea weed.

Hesitant and shy, she shows a new face:
as she grows full she blooms serene, bemused,
unconcerned. She manipulates, a true user.
She's no shade near blue. By no means cool,

she's fevers' degrees away from a chill.
Bare branches web her like grillwork. Crabs
move silently through the water beneath her.

Stars rattle, brittle chips far from a light
source. She's losing light in this battle.
She loses light in this bitter battle for it.

A wind thumps the trees. Dry branches rattle
grey wood. They're bare: their grey bark
consumes light, assuming an endless source.

At best our girl's frail: waning, she's wan.
Chalk white, she rises stiffly, making her dusk
debut nightly, newly pure and white after her
initial flush. Ingénue, she'll blush for the

smallest audience: she'll go all orange for
their applause; then, growing proud, she'll
rise above it. Snob, she'll fall silent, as
though she knows no one's immune to what ails
her. Her waning face's cracks darken like a

china doll's buried for years with the years'
dirt still wedged in her china creases. All
told life's day to day. Life's totally day to
day and the user's the loser. The user loses.

The small orchard's meager crop's no harvest
this year. Ignored, the apples drop piecemeal,
sheer windfall. In a rush the colors come down,
a sheet, a blanket muffling sound. Now
the landscape's sheet-draped, abandoned
this season. The owner's gone south.

Inside shined brass dulls, losing its polish.
The andirons sulk by the cold fireplace.
No one rifles the Almanac on its string on the wall
or rakes the ashes. The halls are cold.

Small creatures take over:
rabbits, squirrels, a mouse.
Grouse and quail share seed pods.
Deer browse on twigs.

These thick mists circle no street lamps.
No parlor's lighted against the dusk.
What rustles the leaves isn't booted or shod,
and over them at night the night crackles with cold.

The stars are put now to no practical usage:
no pilot, sailor, surveyor tells time
or direction or position by them.
They simply twinkle, as the rhyme said;
and if a final ruddy fruit falls with a thud,
who uses it is plural and not human.

Nothing notes the season's shift. What
the night glitters with is not stars or
moon but steel and glass, brass, the hard
knocks of concrete. I coast the surface
of sleep; my eyes deny the street's light.
In the gloom the shadows do not move or
change or dim with rain. At noon they'll
be frail lines: here light is lighter,
here at night dark parts. I might dream

of cobwebbed paste cakes in the baker's
window; I turn that down to dwell on wild
heifer, to hope she's frisking somewhere in
a bell of crisp air and kicking the wind-

fall she dined on. If I woke to find myself
up against an oak trunk I'd follow that
beast's lead: and where light moves we'd
share greed and raid the seed corn feast:
there I'd trade these ears for horns, these
clumsy feet for deft hooves. But I'm sunk
in cement, in exile for no reason: lying
awake in the dark, I'm trying to cope and
wishing these walls would go up in smoke.

Over the rickety bridge to sleep: past
ringed stumps gleaming with dew,
through briars and underbrush,
vines, the rich smell of ripe grapes,
along a road covered with leaves and
shadows of trees that moved
when the moon moved: then

the men in the upstairs room
of the ramshackle church, the musty
damp upholstery, a chair breaking
under my weight, stuffing and springs
leaping out of the cushion, and in the
light of the unshaded lamp one man
smiling at me knowingly, grasping at me,

me the one he'd waited for eagerly,
impatient as a lover, explaining to me
that all he wanted was to show me
what he'd made, shaking something
rattling in my face, jumping
toward me, laughing, "Look!"
The stairs unsafe, the night

crisp and bright, chilled with sweat,
unharmed, outside at last in the cold air,
the steep ravine full of mist,
my inheld breath exhaled at my escape,
the dry crackle of leaves
under my feet and I'm innocent,
innocent, I've done nothing!

V

The Quarry

Robert Schultz

Whether driving trucks and working on road crews led Robert Schultz to write and teach poetry in a university is a question his biographer will have to answer. And did playing baseball and football at Luther College in his home state of Iowa direct him to study seventeenth century poetry at Wroxton College in England? Whatever route he may have taken toward Cornell University, Schultz has recently completed the degrees of Master of Fine Arts and Doctor of Philosophy there. He has written poetry, published in *The Greenfield Review, The Small Farm, Road Apple Review, Cutbank,* and other journals. A chapbook, *Vein Along the Fault,* appeared in 1979. He teaches in the Department of English at Cornell and serves as an editor of *Epoch.* The poems in this anthology provide evidence that Robert Schultz has found his permanent concerns, before his thirtieth year.

The high plateau trickles beginnings.
Granite ripples the outlet creek.
Clear sliding curdles at boulders, hiding

Trout nosing emergent nymphs.
I dip to splash, and gulp cold stones
Of water, pure and baptismal.

Here at their source, I can step across
The oceans, thinking of Vaughan
Who called the Usk his Helicon.

*

In Wales, by Newton, where Vaughan
Heard harps, the Usk begins
Like this mountain feeder: strings of water

Played in splash-pools under the falls.
Here, one night, he saw eternity's
Pure and endless light.

*

When night comes on, and the last
Magenta blackens behind the peaks,
I in my tent begin to hear the kissing

Glasses, cocktail crystal rattling
On silver trays in the water's roiling.
Women's voices bubble in bright

Conversation off among pines.
Laughter spills. Piano music perhaps.
And far in the back, a breaking

Glass, argument raised to
Hysterics just as the wind picks up
The roof. Pines lash when boxcars

Of wind crash by, opening throats
Of wolves. Limbs, needles, a jutting rock,
Anything roughly blade-like slits

The wind. Howling surrounds me.
Curled in nylon, circled by
Tongues, I reach for

Calm, repeating the word consolation.
Consolation, a word to whistle
In darkness, soon falls apart:

Syllables rounded, perfectly
Mute like rock. The peaks still
Carve long howls from the air, and I know,

When quiet water breaks
Into voice on rocks, and wind takes up
Its voice, august in a stand of pines,

Our familiar words, held snug under the tongue,
Puffed with our daily breath,
And rolled in the mouth

Like a drink of water,
Derive from this wilder range
And are wholly strange.

*

Bright red ball
In the pines' low rungs.
All the birds' cacophony.

Antlers dip to the stream.
Birds scrape beaks on the branches.
New, every day, from the root on up.

The sky drops sheer from its outer banks
To my tent-pole tip,
Gripping the objects of sense.

My boots, a pot, the kindling sit
In the morning light, as if
They had not danced all night in the wind.

Sunlight strikes the water
Hard into memory: bright medallion
Of Language older than Greek.

I dip to drink and look
For the women I heard last night
In the creek — something waving

Above the glittering bed, lifting
With grace like a voice,
Gesture so clear and cooling,

Yet not apart from the ripping
Air, shouts from behind the looming
Escarpment, pain extreme of division.

*

Helicon, "the willow mountain," glitters and waves
In memory: willows, "with flexible twigs,"
Suited for weaving —

Thus I invoke, as if the muses,
Fluent voices clear in rapids
High in the Rockies,

To ask for gifts, the skill to weave
My basket tight to carry down this
Water, limpid, cool, to your lips.

With such relief I leave your house
And drive an asphalt road past flooding
Creeks, wet stubble, bushes loused
With catkins and splitting buds. The blood

Cuts loose with the final melt and the heavy
Drinking starts. All our talk rips in the wind,
So many lines of shirts too small for the sky!
Things clamor now. Seeds break and tiny

Fists push up, warning us they mean to climb.
Or are they tongues? There's so much jazz
In the soil we should keep still by the limb
In bloom, green with the latest news.

This is what we are always trying to say.
To pronounce the hole in the page
Where the shoot pokes through, to make
That rip leaf out and put on rings with age.

I've stopped, now, by a field where the twigs
Shrill up in hundreds from last year's stumps,
Redundant, gray, but reeding the wind
So it whistles like a flute or whip.
I will come back and try to tell you of it.

On Forsythia Overhanging a Slate Wall, University Ave., Ithaca, NY

Forsythia sprawls from a central bang.
Branches arc like delight, as if to map
Trajectories of the heart. When the sap
Knocks in its pipes, the yellow blossoms swing
Like suns, brief trumpets loud with their light
Squeezed out from a branch of the void. Suns cool,
Then drop like blossoms or cities into the pool
That can't be ruffled and reflects no light.

This bush shows how, by resistance, lives are built.
Forsythia — slow fountain — drills for the heart,
Taps capillary rills, and pumps rich silt,
Finds rhymes in the leaves' green labs, knots dirt
And sunlight tight, and over this slate wall
Slows water to a lobed and tendrilled fall.

"My soul has gone to live in my eyes, and
like a bold young lady it lolls in those
sunny windows."
                              — Wyndham Lewis

My soul has gone to live in my eyes
And lolls in the sun
And is glad the windows are clean.
Three green leaves still flap on a bush,
Unsinged by its cap of snow.

The soul enjoys a yellow ball
In a snowy lot, the shaking of weeds,
The angle at which a gray shed leans.
Pleasure is loose in a sudden thaw
When the concrete shines.

Cascadilla Place

Some nights I've climbed this hill to overlook
The town's blue light, its glowing tv tubes,
The newscast, our fluorescent sheen of guilt.
I'd fall for the sky's old tricks, or a mouthful

Of cheap champagne, each bubble star-like as
It broke. But tonight this winter rain
Slicks vision to its peak. Diversions fail
And every brittle leaf of the mind spins down.

The shrubs are strung with lenses.
At each twig-end, in a droplet, hangs
A lamppost upside-down, the glazing streets
Around it, quivering on a slender branch.

By a Frozen Lake

Slate chatters underfoot.
Old tablets splinter, chip, unlode
The absence of a fish or crab
We've pinned to the sky with stars.

I throw a pebble dented with the image of a fish
Across the ice. Its clatter echoes off huge
Sturgeons wintered deep
In lake-mud, stiff with cold.

I toss a stone
With a man inside to the moon.
He breaks a crust of sea,
Leaves fish-shaped bootprints, scales

A crater rim
And turns to call to his own
Where ice booms, cracked with tides,
Knits fissured like a skull.

Having flown to the plains of Mars,
Sniffed thin, rusty air, peered far
Over the rim of our own blue
Ball into a desert lot strewn
Thick with rocks without names,
Having measured the red wind's aim
And sifted pink sand for the slightest
Squirm of life, I like the willow best —
Which I find on my shorter strolls —
Because of the way its green tendrils
Twine in a breeze like the twin-
Coiled strands by which I climbed in.

Fire-Eater

On the sun the fiery towers
Hurtle up; bright arcs billow and split,
Blown by genial rage.

The Earth answers
Mildly. Its green corona
Shines on the hills.

And who is happier than I am,
Browsing the lettuces, tasting
The cooled, brittle flames.

The coral snake,
A thread of colored smoke
Among alveoli;
Highways stripe-backed,
Botched with shattered cars;
And, of course, the stars:
Windows we broke diving through —

Like the blonde on the roof of a black sedan,
Reclining in a summer dress, ankles crossed,
Metal rippling out from her shoulders and hips
Like silk. Jewels in her hair, cut glass.

The Lion, Being Hungry,
Throws Himself upon the Antelope

after Henri Rousseau

The lion grins
Deep in the antelope's flank.
Birds wave ribbons of meat.

A leopard, rosette coat and claws, who knows
Her chance will come
Lies hidden in a den of leaves
While the sky goes red around
The orange sun gored on a green palm.

The lion's eyes
Glare blind as teeth.

Still, each leaf hums with a separate light.

And you, Le Douanier, clarinetist to the regimental band,
Could not help
But add, at the antelope's eye,
Your editorial tear.

Of Bottles

Today the wind throws weeks
Across the sky, clouds whirl
Sweet with rain that will
Not fall, and all my strength
Won't push me through.
I look like some insane
Norwegian god, thin blond hair
Bolts from my head
In each odd angle of the wind,
My rumored powers
Silly with disuse.
Everyone is getting drunk
Every day. It seems
A high wind throws their
Sky, hair, brains
That will not fall
Asleep without some emptying
Of bottles.

4:00 AM

for Mark Schrader

The moon falls fast
Around the falling earth.
Cars pass. Blue light
Yaws across the wall like smoke.

Something's called me up. I echo
Through my rooms, a dream
Of blackbirds there until
I nose against a wall, think

Thanks for certain edges,
Little pains, those scars
By which we navigate.
On the stove blue pilots

Witness to the certainties
Of morning: cast iron in the palm,
Black coffee on the tongue, the common sense
Of kitchen talk, the constancy of love.

Led by a small blue flame,
I walk and see the moon slip
Through the telephone wires.
My next dime falls west.

Except for the red-oak's splash,
an occasional jay,
or the breeze
                    sliced
by the sumac leaves,
the trees have been empty for days.

Our vision's cleared.
                    Now we see
all the way to the lake.
                    Light rips
the water at the wave-tips,
cuts bright doors in the town's west edge.

That's where we want to go, Sally,
out to the lake
to cruise on the jingling sparks,
canoe like the fools
we are for the lightning
                    rippling
slowly like fat water snakes on the swells.

        *

Dip oar
and the water whorls at its blade
like a shoulder flexing.
                    We
and the lake pull by.
                    Reflections
quiver, slip with our strokes. The roads
and the trees, we ourselves
fan out in
waves from the prow. Your hair
and a road wind trellised in the limbs.
Where does the body end?

134

*

This is the road I'll take, gone
blond with dust.
                    I'll stroke,
You steer.
            We'll ride on out
that lithe geometry of water lights.

Remember this: we've named the fall
a clearing. Pull
for the bright west edge.

Rocky Ground

I watch the weather spin around
These fields. Clouds roll; we turn and rake
This earth, like love, this rocky ground.

The wind gusts, lightning strolls the clouds,
But no rain falls. I plot rows straight
And watch the weather spin around.

Granite ribs, their veins sown
Rich with ore, gleam spade-struck, grate
In the earth, like love, a rocky ground.

We spade, hoe, rake; try not to count
The hours. While someone plays a three note flute
I watch the weather spin around

And whip up coils of dust that clown
In the rows like crops. Eyes burn. We hate
This earth, this love, the rocky crown

That rings when a hoe hits slate. Soon
Grapes will swirl on hammered stakes.
I watch the weather spin around
This earth, like love, this rocky ground.

The complex leaf
Which a potted palm deploys
Lifts me clear of the chattering

Into the risings
Of each of her parts in the fruit tree,
Grasses, and fern.

I think of the perfect repose
Of an apple filling,
The body that turns, remote;

But only a stack of hollow
Bones can hold the juice so hot
With picture, number, and love —

Electrical, quick, and
Bright in the dark
Of the synapse gap,

It leaps to unite
Seer and seen, lover and beloved.
O sister, forgive me for speaking

This language of disease, of parts
Which break: the synapse, blood, and heart
That swing in a gallows of bones.

Sores in the mouth
Tasting like nails; cancer building
Its city deep in the bone —

This is the world which still
Pretends to offer that garden
Of memory: desert apples,

A circle of hills, spikenard and saffron,
Calamus, balms, and aloes —
All the chief spices, and water running

With light on its back by the palm,
The almonds, the gathering hands.
Where is this garden, sister?

We dream of the perfect
Repose of an apple, broken,
Filling with light.

The Quarry

By gravel light along the quarry road,
Sumac leaves, like longboats,
Oar in the wind.
Cottonwoods and side-oats waver,
Clutching the rim where the breeze steps off
And limestone piles down
Deep in the grassy pool.

Across the strata, drills bit grooves
Where charges slid and fossils
Jumped like fish from stone.

Water seeps through sandstone ribs. Stars
Pour down old light to lakes
Of rattling corn.

Now the moon's up red through dusty willows.
Just another rock, we said, but
Woman-like, my water leans. Recollection
Startles up the taste of iron from the tongue —
I dredge for what I've drowned of you.

When all that weight
Comes down around the voice
I search myself for quick, hard sounds,

Not to make an end,
But leave a line, a vein
Along the fault.

140   ACKNOWLEDGMENTS *continued from page vi*

Abrams, Doug: "The Marshes," POETRY, June 1977, Vol. CXXX., No.
    3. "The Man Who Would Not Speak," WIND/LITER-
    ARY JOURNAL, Vol. 7, No. 24, 1977; "The Conclu-
    sions," WIND/LITERARY JOURNAL, Vol. 7, No. 24,
    1977; "Severance," WIND/LITERARY JOURNAL,
    Vol. 8, No. 28, 1978.

Friend, Barbara: "For Eve," POETRY NORTHWEST, Spring 1975,
    Vol. XVI, No. 1; "Adam's Rib," YANKEE MAGA-
    ZINE, Yankee, Inc., June 1974; "Easter Service," THE
    VIRGINIA QUARTERLY REVIEW, published un-
    der the title, "Easter Mourning," Winter 1975, Vol.
    51, No. 1; "Lullaby," THE POETRY SOCIETY OF
    GEORGIA YEARBOOK, published under the title,
    "Sonnet for a Son and Daughter," Vol. 49, 1973; "Elegy
    for a Lobsterman," POETRY SOCIETY OF AMER-
    ICA, Gassner Prize, 1976; "Mother Goose," THE
    SMITH, December, 1975; "Actress," THE GHENT
    QUARTERLY, Summer, 1975.

Jennings, Kate: "Harvest Moon," POETRY, October, 1976; "Fish
    Store," POETRY, July, 1975; "Late August," WIND/
    LITERARY JOURNAL, Vol. 9, No. 34; "The Closed
    House," THE NORTH AMERICAN REVIEW, Vol.
    260/No. 2/, Summer 1975. "City Dreams," Copyright
    Winter 1972, by Washington and Lee University, re-
    printed from SHENANDOAH: THE WASHING-
    TON AND LEE UNIVERSITY REVIEW; "The
    Alchemist," Copyright Fall 1974 by Washington and Lee
    University, reprinted from SHENANDOAH: THE
    WASHINGTON AND LEE UNIVERSITY RE-
    VIEW; "Stock Pot" and "Rural Route," THE AMERI-
    CAN SCHOLAR; "Sunday Afternoon in November,"
    SOUTHERN POETRY REVIEW, Spring, 1980 (XX:1).
    "Fish Store," "Garlic," "All Souls' Day," "The Closed
    House," and "The Alchemist" appeared in 1976 in *Second
    Sight*, an Iron Mountain Press Poetry Chapbook, IRON
    MOUNTAIN PRESS, Copyright 1976.

Schultz, Robert: "Leaving," THE SMALL FARM, Nos. iv-v (double issue: October, 1976 and March, 1977); "Cascadilla Place," THE GREENFIELD REVIEW, Vol. 6, Nos. iii-iv (double issue: Spring, 1978); "By a Frozen Lake," ROAD APPLE REVIEW, Spring, 1976; "The Lion, Being Hungry, Throws Himself Upon the Antelope," RAINY DAY, Winter, 1977; "Of Bottles," THE REMINGTON REVIEW, Vol. 5, November, 1977; "The Quarry," SOU'WESTER, Vol. 6, No. ii, Summer, 1978. All of these poems and "Trail Guide," "On Forsythia Overhanging a Slate Wall, Ithaca, N.Y.," "Having Flown to the Plains of Mars," "Fire-Eater," and "Rocky Ground" were published in *Vein Along the Fault*, a Laueroc Press Chapbook, THE LAUEROC PRESS, Copyright 1979. "Invocation," "In Mourning," "Sight," "Reply to Bliss," and "4:00 AM" appear in this volume for the first time: Copyright 1980, Robert Schultz.

Contributors

A. R. AMMONS is Goldwin Smith Professor of Poetry at Cornell University. His first book of poetry, *Ommateum*, appeared in 1955. In 1973 *Collected Poems* won the National Book Award. *Sphere: The Form of a Motion* received the Bollingen Prize in 1975.

JOHN HOLLANDER first published *A Crackling of Thorns*, which was chosen by W. H. Auden in 1958 for the Yale Series of Younger Poets. *Visions from the Ramble* was published in 1965, *The Head of the Bed*, 1973, *Reflections on Espionage*, 1976. He teaches at Yale University.

JOSEPHINE JACOBSEN has written poetry (including *The Animal Inside* and *The Shade-Seller*, short stories *(A Walk with Raschid and Other Stories)*, and criticism *(The Testament of Samuel Beckett* and *Genet and Ionesco: Playwrights of Silence* with William R. Mueller).

JOSEPHINE MILES recently retired from teaching at the University of California at Berkeley. Her first book of poetry was *Lines at Intersection*, published in 1939. *Poems New and Selected* appeared in 1974, *Coming to Terms* in 1979. Among her critical works is *The Continuity of Poetic Language*.

ROBERT PENN WARREN is the author of thirty-three books. *All the King's Men* (1946) was awarded the Pulitzer Prize for Fiction; *Promises* (1957) won the Pulitzer Prize for Poetry and the National Book Award. In 1967 he received the Bollingen Prize for *Selected Poems: New and Old, 1923–1966*. He received his third Pulitzer Prize for *Now and Then — Poems 1976–1978*. His latest publication is *Being Here — Poetry 1977–1980*.

The text of this book was set in Janson, a Dutch type style.
The paper is Warren Olde Style Wove Offset, which meets
library specifications.

Composed, Printed, and
Bound by Kingsport Press
Kingsport, Tennessee